IN GALLOWAY

Matthew Curry

with illustrations by Miranda Paris

CARNFORTH PRESS

IN GALLOWAY

ISBN 978-0-9564874-1-4

First Published 2010 by
Carnforth Press
6 St John's Road
Old Trafford
Manchester M16 7GX

Printed in Great Britain by
www.direct-pod.com

IN GALLOWAY

At Wood of Cree the Cree is frozen over.
And last night's snow rests on the ice.
Wide and flat. Eerie stillness.
And somewhere underneath, the fluid river.

Safety

On the more remote of these walks you must take basic precautions for your own safety. You need to leave word somewhere of exactly where you are going and when, you need to provide for the fact that the weather can change very fast.

What you must take, as a minimum: sturdy footwear, waterproofs, relevant O.S. Explorer Map 318, 319, or 312, or similar; a waterproof cover for your map; food and drink and means to keep warm and dry, should you have to spend the night in the open; compass, and know how to use it; take your mobile, but be aware that there are many places where you won't get coverage at all.

Advice

Although the author has taken care to ensure the accuracy of this guide, facts on the ground can change. The route sketches are not to scale – you also need an O.S. map with you.

Acknowledgements

The author has found useful the book 'The Galloway Hills: A Walkers' Paradise', by George Brittain. Some of the routes that the author includes, he first encountered with that book.

Contents

Illustrations

Buchan Hill

To get to the start:

From Newton Stewart take the A714 north, turn right at
Bargrennan, signposted to Glentrool. At Glentrool village, turn
right, signposted to Loch Trool. Go straight on past Stroan
Bridge visitor centre a further couple of miles, to the Loch Trool
car park, which is in two parts.

The Walk:

From the top car park, follow the continuation of the road,
which takes you winding down to Buchan Bridge. Immediately
after the bridge take the footpath, left, which takes you up the
east side of Buchan Burn. Stay fairly close to the burn, as you
want to ascend the less steep west side of the hill. After half a
mile or so, start to bear away from the stream, heading round
the back (to the north of) the steep Black Gairy of the hill's
south side. From the summit of Buchan Hill (493m) you can
head back the way you came or alternatively head west north
west fairly gently down to Loch Valley, where you pick up the
Gairland Burn path back round the east and south sides of
Buchan Hill. This is my favoured route, as Gairland Burn is
particularly beautiful. Great area for a picnic. The path returns
you to the road you left, just a short distance beyond Buchan
Bridge.

Time and Difficulty:

The circular version is a walk of about four miles. The other about three miles. Allow a good two hours for either. The main difficulty is in finding a sensible way up, avoiding the steep outcrops. Even though it's not as high as many of these hills, the steep last third is testing, and remember that any route without a given path inevitably takes longer.

Buchan Hill

Loch Valley

Gairland Burn

Buchan Hill

Buchan Burn

Start JP

Loch Trool

N

On Buchan Hill

The sound of my boots is loud
in the crunchy, days old snow.
When I stop I hear only
a heavy forestry vehicle
working invisibly in the long distance.
I stop next to stand out
on a natural, flat, stone promontory
with a boulder sitting on it
just off from the Gairland Burn path
on the footslopes of Buchan Hill -
if a hill can have footslopes.

I'm aching all over
from yesterday's exertions,
but especially for some reason in my shoulders.
I think it must be the tension
of the ice-hobbling gait,
the muscles' constant readiness
to readjust instantly.
Anyway I cut
a proper Romantic figure
on my own with my stick
standing surveying the scene below.

Erratic boulders, they call them,
deposited at random
by the retreating glaciers
of the last ice age.
Before geology opened up

vast new temporal vistas,
Wordsworth mentioned them -
in *Resolution and Independence.*
The old man appears to have appeared
in the same unexplained
and hence seemingly
meaningful way.
Wordsworth knows it only seems so.

I feel like I'm in a painting.
Endued with sense.
Loch Trool with the ice touching,
just kissing
across the middle,
and the white-dusted hills.

The next time I stop
I have been working along a dyke
under a steep outcrop.
Movement. I stop carefully, then look up. See the deer.
A female. And now that I have stopped she stops.
I have been moving across and underneath her.
When I move, she moves twice as far off.
When I stop, she stops.
I suppose she's hard wired this way
to avoid predators.
Not programmed to deal with those
who kill without touching.
She knows she can keep away from me.
She looks heavy, perhaps with foal.
Then I see another, smaller deer,
following her, and then two more.

They are moving off now, steadily
to the top of the hill.
I walk on, below where they were
and from where they were,
tucked over the grassy knoll,
not President Kennedy's motorcade,
not Lee Harvey Oswald's bullet, but a coarse
grunt almost a bark, sudden and short,
a sound that hits you in the chest
as much as the ear.
Comes into view now towards me,
antlerless stag,
new ones just starting, pointing up
no longer than his ears. Mouth open.
I start walking again.
He moves off following the others,
a patient escort.
I get my binoculars and watch the ease
with which they pick their way,
careful with their footing,
the smallest lifting her right hind leg
more slowly than her others
and placing it down more slowly.
But for now, she keeps up with her mother.

The stag stops, and barks down again,
and the valley shakes,
my rib cage vibrates.

I had thought to go round to Gairland Burn,
maybe even get to Loch Neldricken,
but I am aching still and I know

my car's front wheels were spinning where I left it.
And seeing the deer is enough.

As I return, the stag,
changed without his dark mistletoe,
his erotic charge,
is on the skyline.
A family man.
Undramatic and helpless.
At the mercy of guns.

I gather flat stones where I can,
and sticks and bits of bracken,
and at the empty car park I fill
an empty plastic bag I have with grit.
Back at the car, left with others
on the side of the road
at the foot of a sharp incline
too risky on this ice,
I stuff them all
behind and in front of the front wheels
and it's just enough
to get me out of the hole I'd spun.

After a day of sun,
the ice holds more danger.
Only the ruts keep me on the road
and I attain Stroan Bridge
from where the roads are gritted,
nervy and more alive, and see
the fast Water of Minnoch,
almost, almost completely locked.

Buchan Bridge

At the bridge the big pool
is still lucid.
Above it the ice accumulates.
Cauliflowers of ice, mangrove roots,
a small sidepool made of criss-cross needles.

But Buchan Burn is still viable,
mushrooms of, slept-in sheets of ice
notwithstanding.
Here, only volume and movement
do not freeze.

Above the barren pool
hang harpoons,
patient as the cold.
Not even dripping.

Wood of Cree

To get to the start:

From Newton Stewart town centre, drive across the bridge over
the Cree, onto the B7079, heading east from the main town
centre of Newton Stewart. Take the first turn left, signed
Minigaff. Turn left again, where it's signed Wood of Cree. This
takes you over a bridge over Penkiln Burn, and then on up a
beautiful run of about four miles along the east side of the River
Cree. The car park is on the left, immediately after the
humpbacked Cordorcan Bridge.

The Walk:

Cross the road from the car park, and go up the obvious path.
These woods are important as they are some of the most
ancient in Scotland. Managed by the RSPB, there is a donation
box after about a hundred yards. Go on up alongside the rushing
Cordorcan Burn and the steep and narrow little gorge it has cut
for itself. Soon you choose between two paths, a short loop
which stays in woodland, or a longer route, a couple of miles in
total, which takes you out onto scrubland above the woods.
With kids in tow I tend to stick to the smaller one. There's a
bench at the top of the larger loop which makes a good picnic
spot.

We find deciduous woods make great walks for kids. There's a
comforting sense of enclosure without it being claustrophobic.
They can pick up sticks. If it rains heavily, you're not too
exposed. There's a deep sense of at-homeness which the adults

feel a little of, but which the children just seem naturally to tap into. I have seen deer up in the scrubland part, but only once, alone, in winter. The noise inherent in a family outing makes it a lot less likely.

On the way back down, stop at a viewing point (be careful, there are very steep drops), from where you can see out and down to the broad, slow-moving Cree, and also back alongside you see a high wide, straggly waterfall. The path then takes you back to the bottom.

Two more things: There's a small lay-by further along the road, just below that waterfall, and a path you can follow to get right to the foot of it. Also, from the car park, there's a signposted short path to a platform overlooking the River Cree, from where you can sometimes see otters. It's a peaceful spot, well worth spending some time, even if, like me, you never glimpse an otter. The Cree was completely frozen over last time I was there, the ice covered in snow, creating a flat white expanse. Near dusk or near dawn, on a still day, is the advice for getting the best chance of spotting an otter.

Time and Difficulty:

A lovely, not too strenuous walk, ideal for kids, or a picnic, or if your legs are aching after a big walk the day before. The short loop is about a mile, the longer loop two miles.

Waterfall

The self-same
turns and tells,
stammers lambeg thunder,
peat, gold, brown.

In thick spate
plunges to repeat a phrase,
which hits and
holds you under.

And I am again,
who last year saw
the same stream,
the self-same.

23

Castramont Wood

(Spelt variously on different maps and signs as Castramont, Carstramon, Carstramont)

To get to the start:

From Gatehouse-of-Fleet, take the Laurieston road, which is the last left turn as you head east out of Gatehouse. There is a celtic cross war memorial at the junction. Drive out past Gatehouse golf club. (Visitors are welcome here, and there's a really challenging nine hole course set in wonderful scenery – if it's clear you will see the gorgeous Fleet valley, the Fleet estuary, and Cairnsmore of Fleet in the distance, from various vantage points as you go round.)

Soon after, take the left fork in the road. This takes you through rolling farmland and on into woodland. There are several bays along the way for parking, but the favoured spot is just before a left turn which would take you down to the bridge over the Fleet at Nether Rusko. There's ample parking, and the path up is clear from here.

The Walk:

The path soon divides and you can go a slow ascent left, with views over a large country house and its grounds, or follow the main route up and right, taking you to the top of the tree-covered hill. There are many variations, since paths go off all over, but this main direct route up is a good one if you have kids in tow, since once you get them up to the top you can relax a little, the whingeing should be over! The path then turns left, through a small clearing planted with new oaks some years ago, and on along the slowly descending hilltop. There are many huge and spooky trees, the product of long abandoned coppicing. There are old charcoal burning platforms tucked away here and there on the hillside. You may well hear woodpeckers, and see the odd deer. (I should say that I had been assuring my wife of the presence of deer here for seven years before we saw one together.) The tiny streams and huge ferns are of a scale just right to kindle a child's sense of wonder. In spring, you get great carpets of bluebells, in summer the ferns are high and green, in autumn brown that in an evening light glows bronze. If you follow this path to its finish it comes out at the road you parked on but much further down. If you turn left when it meets another similar sized path coming up, that takes you back to the car.

If you're going back to or via Gatehouse, see a different route by going left down over the Fleet at Nether Rusko (there's a good fly-fishing pool just yards away, from which I saw a big salmon reeled twenty-five or so years ago - fishing permits are available in Gatehouse). You go up very steeply, then left again onto the road which follows the opposite side of the Fleet valley back to Gatehouse.

Time and Difficulty:

For adults of average fitness, it's a nice leisurely walk. If you follow the favoured loop described, allow say an hour. You can easily extend that, as there are paths all over these woods.

Waterfall at Pool Ness

To get to the start:

From Gatehouse-of-Fleet take the B796, the old Gatehouse Station road. Travelling west through the town, it's a right turn just before The Ship Inn. Follow this road winding up through the beautiful Fleet Valley, the wooded Doon of Castramont over to the right. Go straight on past the turn down to Nether Rusko, pass the renovated Rusko Tower. You emerge from the woodland onto moors. Take care now, there are often sheep on the road. Soon there's a white cottage on the left (Upper Rusko Cottage). Park just after it, on the hard standing to the right.

The Walk:

The path goes down from opposite the cottage. Across a field, then short and steep past a barn, to the waterfall below. A good place for a picnic, overlooking the waterfall, and Pool Ness below it. On your way down you passed a path going off to the right, which you can go back up and take now, following the Big Water of Fleet further down its valley. You can either then turn back and retrace your steps, or follow it right round and up to the road your car's parked on.

Time and Difficulty:

The way down to the waterfall is steep at times. Because the climb's at the end, I've found myself carrying the kids up on several occasions. Very relaxing down by the river, where there's often a heron, still as a hieroglyphic, waiting.

You could get down to the falls and back in fifteen minutes, but you could spend a whole day up here. On hot days bathers sometimes come to the pool beneath the waterfall. The peaty water, straight of the hills, is always very cold!

Big Water of Fleet Viaduct

To get to the start:

From Gatehouse-of-Fleet take the B796, the old Gatehouse Station road. Travelling west through the town, it's a right turn just before The Ship Inn. This road takes you up the Fleet Valley. Note Castramont Woods on the hill to the right, then on up, past the turn down to Nether Rusko bridge, past Rusko Tower, on (watching out for sheep on the road) past Upper Rusko Cottage, and after another mile, there's a junction where the old Gatehouse Railway Station was, and you turn right here to take the track down to the Big Water of Fleet Viaduct. If it's clear, you may have already spotted it, over to the right as you drove up, looking like something out of Harry Potter, nestled below and to the east of the craggy Clints of Dromore. Take it slowly, the track is bumpy! You may need to open and close gates on the way down. Parking is just through the arches of the viaduct.

The Walk:

Follow the path up to the old railway line and take a nice flat walk along it, under the Clints of Dromore (283m). Amazing to think that most of the freight and people going to and from the Northern part of Ireland used to come this way. Surely the route should be re-opened. Dalbeattie, Castle Douglas, Newton Stewart, have all suffered from the lack of this essential link.

A more adventurous walk is to climb to the top of the Clints (take care - there are several sensible easy routes up them, but there are some parts only suitable for rock-climbers), and then walk along the tops of them, dropping down at the end, returning via the grassy slopes beneath them.

(You can use this walk along the tops of the Clints of Dromore as a start for an ascent of Cairnsmore of Fleet, an alternative to the popular route I've described in this book... It's on my to-do list!)

(One walk we did from the viaduct has gone down in family folklore as the trek from hell. In teeming rain with whingeing kids we walked on up the forestry track towards Loch Grannoch. It is a long tedious walk with nothing to see, hemmed in by pines either side, punctuated by the odd wasteland of stumps. The kids are not impressed when I now say, on a rainy day, let's take a nice walk up through that lovely forest track to Loch Grannoch. So if you are tempted to do Cairnsmore from here, my advice is don't do the big loop some recommend, via Loch Grannoch, go straight up via the Clints and the Doors of Cairnsmore. I've taken against Loch Grannoch.)

Time and Difficulty:

Walking along the disused railway is easy going. You choose how far and how fast to go. Going up the Clints is a short sharp bit of hill walking, perfect if you've only got an hour or two spare.

Cambret Hill

To get to the start:

Travelling west from Gatehouse-of-Fleet, take the A75 for about
two miles, then on a long sweeping bend near the shoreline,
take the right turn signed Skyreburn. After half a mile or so take
the left fork. About three miles along this narrow moorland road
(watch out for sheep), there's a track joins it from the right. This
is the Old Military Road coming up from Gatehouse, via Anwoth.
Built in the 18th Century, it connected Gatehouse to Creetown,
then known as Ferrytown of Cree. (Creetown's location has even
older military connections, since in 1300 the main English
garrison was stationed at a village there called Creth. It is from
here that troops were sent out to try to capture Robert Bruce).
Continue, now on the course of that old road, known here as
the Corse of Slakes Road. A mile or so further on, there is a road
leading off left, up to the masts and satellites. Park at the foot of
this road.

The Walk:

Walk up the track to the top of Cambret Hill (351m). Great views
on a clear day, to Cairnharrow (456m) and the sea beyond, to
the Isle of Man, and, turning northwards, the huge array of hills.
If it's really clear, south east you see the Lake District.

Time and Difficulty:

This is a really easy way to get some fantastic views. Five or ten
minute walk to the top. And it's a nice drive through the hills.

Afterwards, you can drive on round to Creetown, via Billy Diamond's Bridge, imagining the old military hardware trundling on, or head back towards Gatehouse.

Add on:

If you're going back in the Gatehouse direction, a good option is to combine the trip with a stop at Anwoth Old Kirk, a beautiful little ruin in a tranquil vale. Back to the A75, turn left, then take the next left, signed Anwoth. In half a mile, after passing the current church, you can park by the ruin. Look for the gravestone with the story of the 'murderously shot' local covenanter. And see if you can find the gravestone carved with the following lines:

'Pause, traveller, as you pass by,
As you are now, so once was I,
As I am now so you shall be,
Therefore prepare to follow me.'

The place has a wonderful mood all of its own. It was the kirk of Samuel Rutherford, author of Lex Rex, which argued, as the title suggests, that the Law should be King, not the other way around.

Via their influence on the likes of the philosopher John Locke, these precepts from the man who preached in this tiny place influenced the men who drafted the American constitution.

There's a path from Anwoth Old Kirk leading up through larch woods, to Rutherford's Monument (80m), from where you have great views of the Fleet Estuary.

Another add on:

While you're in the area, you could visit Cairn Holy. Take the A75 west for about four miles. Turn right at Kirkdale, follow sign to Cairn Holy. (Alternative scenic route: Go west on A75 for only two miles. Soon after you pass Newton farm on your left, turn off to the right, signposted Laggan and Laggan Outdoor. The narrow road goes up past Laggan, and you can stop for great views of the Fleet Estuary and Wigtown Bay. The road drops down through woods, over a hairpin bridge, and just before it reaches the A75 again, take a hard right back and up, which takes you to Cairn Holy. There are two sites, the lower one being the more impressive, with its chambered tomb, concave facade, and portal stones. Like Anwoth, this place has a very distinctive feel. Apparently, the sun rises at the spring equinox exactly on a notch in a hill to the east, flooding light straight into the entrance to the chamber. But what makes the place special to me is the particular quality of the view down to the sea from here. For a moment, you might be a bronze age man looking down.

Anwoth

The bull in the rushy field
stands still.

I look out through the airy
window of the kirk.

Its roof an ungated
field of sky.

The hinges gone,
here a grassy floor.

Yew trees out there
stretch up,

calm amongst the graves,
the lush humps and bumps.

There are yellow irises
pointing heavenwards.

The silence slowly fills.

Each lichened stone.
Each carved letter.

Kirroughtree Forest

To get to the start:

From Newton Stewart take the A75 eastbound. Turn left at Palnure, also signposted Kirroughtree Visitor Centre. Follow signs to the centre, less than a mile from the A75.

The Walks:

There are three way-marked forest routes, ideal for a family walk. Clear paths all the way.

Time and Difficulty:

Relatively gentle walks. An hour or two's leisurely stroll. There are some small climbs, the routes are well thought out and give plenty of visual variety. Woods, a lake, a dam, a fast-running burn.

Wigtown Walk

To get to the start:

Park in the centre of Wigtown.

The Walk:

Walk down Main Street, go to the left of the town hall, down Church Lane. You can go into the graveyard, where, towards the far side, you can find the martyr's grave. Then continue down the road past the church. At the bottom, turn right to follow the old railway track path. Good views of the distant Cairnsmore of Fleet. There's a boarded path out across to the martyrs stake. (Apparently, two women, Margaret Wilson in her 20s and Margaret McLachlan aged 63, were executed near here. They were tied to stakes and drowned by the incoming tide. Most likely it was in one of the tidal channels of the river Bladnoch. Covenanters, they had refused to say 'God save the king'. The older woman was tied lower down, in the hope that the younger, seeing her drown, would relent. She didn't.) Returning, continue along the railway path which brings you to the old harbour area. This whole area is good for bird watching, and there's supposed to be a pair of ospreys about. I'm no twitcher, I have only seen the graceful herons here. At the harbour you extend the walk along this path before coming back, or straightaway turn right up what becomes Harbour Rd. This road takes you back up to the town.

Time and Difficulty:

This is a leisurely half hour walk. If you linger at the churchyard and the martyrs' stake, call it an hour.

Add ons:

As Scotland's Book Town, Wigtown is full of bookshops to browse round.

Bladnoch Distillery, Scotland's most southerly, is just half a mile away at Bladnoch, on the (you guessed it) river Bladnoch. It's a lovely river, with a good reputation for salmon fishing.

Four miles west of Wigtown, on the B733, there is the bronze age Torhouse stone circle. Parking for a couple of cars. The circle is of a type more often seen in north east Scotland and in Ireland. Legend has it that it is the tomb of King Galdus.(But then some say that this same Corbredus Galdus, who fought the Romans, was interred at Cairn Holy after being killed in a battle on the banks of the river Cree ..)

Bladnoch Ice

After the ice melted here
more came down.

Slid past, slow and sombre,
drew my gaze downstream.

Silent and steady,
with unearthly grandeur,

like the funeral of a great man,
moving down from the higher reaches.

Bladnoch Swans

This morning,
my things all packed
and ready to leave.

The winter sun
strong and low
through the window.

Two swans there,
on the Bladnoch,
a confirmation ,

dipping their heads together
in the black water
amongst the patchy ice.

St. Ninian's Cave

To get to the start:

From Newton Stewart take the A714 south. Follow signs to
Whithorn. At the south end of Whithorn, (not Isle of Whithorn),
follow signs to St. Ninian's Cave.

The Walk:

From the car park (which was pay and display when we were
there), the path takes you round farm buildings, then down
through woods to a stony beach. The cave is at the far end of
the cove. Look for the old crosses carved into the stone of the
entrance. You can see why St. Ninian spent time here.
Wonderfully secluded from humanity, and at the same time
exposed to the full bant of the Irish Sea. We saw seals bobbing
up in the surf. And a hare on the path down.

Time and Difficulty:

It's only half a mile or so down to the cove. The path is clear
and steady, if muddy at times.

Add on:

While you're near the end of the Machars Peninsula, the Isle of
Whithorn is well worth a visit. Harbour, couple of pubs, St.
Ninian's Chapel.

And Whithorn Priory Museum, in Whithorn. Some wonderful carved stone, including the Latinus Stone and the Monreith Cross.

The Hare

On the way down to St. Ninian's cave
I saw a hare.
The first time I have ever seen a hare.
It happened to me at the age of thirty-five
or so
with you and the kids in tow,
and at the time I didn't think it meant much more
than any other event-

and the boys pretended they saw, but they didn't see.

Only now that you have left
and I don't know where you or they are –
and I know that you saw-

Only now does it come to me
what it meant.

Merrick

To get to the start:

From Newton Stewart take the A714 north, turn right at
Bargrennan, signposted to Glentrool. At Glentrool village, turn
right, signposted to Loch Trool. Go straight on past Stroan
Bridge visitor centre a further couple of miles, to the Loch Trool
car park, which is in two parts.

The walk:

A clear path heads off up from the upper car park. The path
takes you up steeply initially, following the course of Buchan
Burn. The path opens out amongst felled forestry in a small vale
before Culsharg, a small bothy. Up again steeply through
forestry and out onto the slopes of Benyellary. The path meets a
wall and follows it, right, to the summit of Benyellary (719m).
Keep following this wall, across the Neive of the Spit (take care,
steep sides to your right). Once across onto the slopes of
Merrick, the path departs from the wall, heading right, north
east, to the summit of Merrick (843m), the highest point in the
south of Scotland. Return the way you came up.

Time and Difficulty:

It's a long slog, but you can do as much or as little of it as you
want. People's fitness and stamina obviously vary hugely , but
someone of average fitness should expect to go up and down in
four to five hours. However, always allow plenty of extra
daylight time, just in case.

Merrick

↑N

Merrick

wall

● Benyellary

● Culsharg

Buchan Burn

Start
P

Loch Trool

47

Merrick

I had done the Merrick climb before
with my eldest daughter.
It is the most popular climb
in the south of Scotland,
and the highest peak.
My younger brother
was the first in the family,
scaling it with his mates as a young man,
and some years later I thought we'd have a go.

The path goes all the way to the top
from the car park at Loch Trool.
Coming from Newton Stewart
you turn off the 714 at Bargrennan
like the English Army did
except they didn't have 4x4s or mountain bikes
they had horses,
right again at Glentrool Village
and go straight on at the Stroan Bridge car park.
You park near Bruce's Stone,
a monument erected above Loch Trool
over the water from the site
of his successful attack
on a much larger English sortie
sent out from the main garrison
based near modern day Creetown - then called Creth .
And they thought they'd cornered him
on the 31st March 1307,
Passion Sunday, but he'd cornered them,

they were strung out fifteen hundred strong
in single file
on a narrow track
on the steep southern side of Loch Trool.
Some of Bruce's three hundred men
stopped and blocked the path
while the others rolled down boulders and threw rocks,
captured many English and only a few escaped,
scarpered back to Creetown.

Anyway before the time my daughter and I
made it to the summit of Merrick,
the previous year we'd turned back short
from the top of Benyellary
which you reach on your way up,
and a year before that,
me, my wife and the two boys,
the younger one in the backpack,
had only got as far as Culsharg
on a hot August day.

And when my daughter and I did complete it,
all the first part of the walk was in sheeting rain
and she'd wanted to turn back
with pains in her back and legs, etcetera,
and I had trickling drops of cold rain down my neck
and we were only in trainers, shorts and cagools,
and we never got to see much but felt great.

We met, on our descent,
a serious pair of hikers heading up,
totally wrapped in Goretex,

even gloves and gaiters,
and ski poles and proper walking boots
and bulbous back-packs with
maybe a tent or God knows what.
They had paused to draw on waterproof leggings
and were just adjusting the pieces of string
under their obligatory beards
as we sauntered past pretending our legs weren't jelly,
the skin of our legs soaked and our shorts and hair,
as we sauntered past I'll never forget
their look of astonishment and mild
disapproval
which transmuted even as it appeared
into a normal and hearty 'hallo',
as we tumbled shambolically but energetically
past
and I whispered a quiet little dig at their expense
because I had felt momentarily admonished.

But this is me on my own,
a family man, empty and free.
Having opened the tailgate to don my boots,
I locked the car and with knapsack and ashplant
I slunk off up the obvious path.

During the first short climb I always turn back
and look at Loch Trool below
and at Mulldonoch on the far side
down which Robert Bruce and his bandits
rolled those terrorist stones.
The whole landscape now is so civil,
cultivated and under control,

the pines and the sheep-cropped hills
the peace of the loch and the peace of the burns,
stone dykes and fences and paths
(think of the man-hours in those dykes)
so civil, and its more formal quality does appeal -
but it's hard to really picture the brutal scene
the desperate and metal violence,
the isolation of the spot
no mettled road or car park
or O.S. maps in plastic, or public information board,
or advice not to leave valuables in your car.
No covenanter's grave no reformation at all
no mountain bike routes or pine trees.
But Buchan Hill was there and Craignaw
and Craiglee and the Rig of the Jarkness
but I wonder what their names were then,
if they had names.

And the streams and the rivers were there
a bit higher
and hairy men with their balls full,
and waterfalls holding their form
mesmeric
and after the daytime the darkness.

I always stop, as I say,
I always stop and look.
The world doesn't fit one style.
The world is the strangest things jammed together,
juxtaposed.

Soon after, as the path moves to shadow Buchan Burn

you see, and that day I saw
and you hear, and that day I heard,
a waterfall.
There is a rowan tree near the path just before it
and you can stand with sprawling falls,
the oxygenating water framing the tree,
the mountain ash,
and this day in September its berries were bright,
not bright, warmly glowing,
and they hung in the sound,
the dreamsound and mesmer of the falls.

Something like embarrassment,
but not as powerful,
breaks the moment, and I move on.
It's a kind of default setting which says
'No-one is watching
but if someone were watching,
if I were at home in the city,
staring still at something for this long in public,
in a dream,
someone might be tempted to contact the authorities,
wondering if I've missed my medication'.
Anyway, whatever it is, I move on.
But the scene remains,
full of the light and sound
of a long exposure.

Into the dark and dank and closeness of forest,
fungus and needles, and the thought from childhood
that there's something just behind the just behind,
and then out onto a small, felled floodplain of Buchan Burn

not a geographer's floodplain perhaps
more a flat niche in the hills next to the stream,
a snug and eerie spot,
the lines of grey stumps and bits of branches,
and the few poles like battle standards.
Culsharg, a small old halt for shepherds, reels up,
and the vale is hemmed in neatly
by Buchan Hill and the Fell of Eschoncan,
and Bennan and Craignine, and the way forward
by the Braes of Mulgarvie.
It is a place full of the peace of death
and the peace before life
which are one and the same,
but being alive it can only be fleetingly glimpsed,
only fleetingly almost glimpsed -
the sight of a pair of buzzards gliding
gives me a great excuse to prolong the sense,
circling on an updraft,
surely they take pleasure in their finesse,
as a dolphin in a bow wave must,
winding and widening above the silent valley,
this immense gyroscope turning
the sun minute in the spiral arm,
and all of that buzzard hardly visible to me,
the clouds of electrons the curve of a beak
the differential equations,
and the galaxy a mere speck -
but the buzzard sees all the world it needs,
and swoops on movement in the still vale.

Beyond Culsharg, a broad forestry
highway of hardcore

cuts across the path, and a works caravan
looks like it just slid off to the side,
having landed from nowhere.
There is a concrete culvert for Whiteland Burn,
strong enough to take the timber wagons -
this is productive, managed land.

A long steep going up a muddy path
I emerge into changed weather -
the clouds are coming down as I go up,
a fell runner passes, and I feel a little shame
at my heavy breathing,
but when he reappears five minutes later
explaining breathily it's too wet up there today,
I feign an easy acknowledgment
and try to send a hiker's steady gaze.

Looking at the 1 to 25000 O.S. map,
it occurs to me that the Dungeon Range
looks like an old distorted map of Great Britain,
perhaps a Scottish map,
since in it Scotland is expanded,
and the area of the O.S. map where I am now
would be north of the Sluice of Loch Enoch,
the border, old and different,
is marked along Pulskaig Burn,
and strange continents are fused on both sides.

I decide I have spent too much time on my own.

Yomping on now in gathering rain,
the path goes up to a wall,

then follows that wall
all the way over Benyellary.
It is a long lump, the thumb of The Awful Hand,
named because together, the hills in the range
form what looks like a deformed hand.

Three women descending
one of them pretty, young and fit.
Her mother, I assume, comments that it's
wet up there and you can't see much.
I smile a knowing fatalistic smile
and shrug a knowing fatalistic shrug
and grunt assent, all these
at the same time aren't I clever,
a bit too much like a hairy man
with his balls full,
but my knapsack and inoffensive, hiker's
'sorry to have bounded into your living room like this' look
save me.

The wall helps shelter from the wind that's got up
but it's a wide muddy thin stream of a path.
I stuff my sarnies and swig my juice
on top of Benyellary without a view,
and continue along the Neive of the Spit where I can see down
over the almost sheer Scars of Benyellary
into a deep bowl pitted with rocks
a smooth shape
the sort of shape you make
if you put your non withered hands together
to hold as much water as they will -
thumbs clamped and round for edges,

little fingers crossing slightly,
the ends of the other fingers turned almost vertical.
And I am walking along the tops of those fingers
along a narrow path next to a dyke.
A few sheep have ludicrously chosen here
of all the places in their broad world
to chew a bit of grass.

Continuing north west, sighted perhaps fifty yards ahead.
From all other sides, the Merrick is steep.
Today the summit is an anti-climax
I can see only hints of steep drops,
peer into the Howe of the Cauldron
but only see the rim,
and mist like steam.
And I've seen the wide panorama on a clear day
so I know what I'm missing.
But this is just my fettling day,
having driven up from Manchester this morning,
so I turn and return.
On reflection
it is wonderful and strange
to know what's there but not see it,
like the stars all day lost in brightness.

My wife and our children are in Spain.
The light is hard and bouncy on the pool.
And slow like David Hockney shows it.

A map helps, a photo helps.
But it doesn't give you what is there.

Kirriereoch

To get to the start:

From Newton Stewart take the A714 north. Turn right at
Bargrennan, signposted Glentrool. At the village of Glentrool, go
straight on, signposted to Straiton. After about six miles, turn
right at Kirriereoch, the road very soon crosses the Water of
Minnoch, and you park at a picnic area just over this bridge.

The Walk:

Follow the track on ignoring the sign to Kirriereoch Loch and
then the one to Kirriereoch Farm. Ignore also the right turn soon
after, and the left turn after that, signed Tarfessock. Walk on
right down this forestry track, eventually crossing Pillow Burn.
Soon after, take the right turn (a continuation of the old track),
where a newish forestry track goes on and left. The forestry
layout, and usage of tracks changes over time. The guide I was
using was clearly written before this last new track was put in,
and I ended up wasting quite a bit of time starting to circle
Tarfessock before I checked my map. Basically you need to take
the track which ends quite close to where Cross Burn first enters
forestry. There is a small area of hard standing at the end of this
track. The O.S. map shows this track continuing as a forest ride,
a wide break in the forest, but it didn't look like that to me. My
old guidebook wanted me to find a path going up Tarfessock
(697m) from the end of the forestry and then go down and up
to Kirriereoch (786m). This may well be there, but I decided,
given the mismatch between what I could see, and both the
map and the old guide, to simply climb Kirriereoch, and to do so

by following something definite on the map. So follow a short ride down to Cross Burn, find a place to cross it, and soon emerge at a fence, a very clearly marked black line on the map, which tracks up Cross Burn and continues all the way up to the saddle between Tarfessock and Kirriereoch. So my route is to follow that fence all the way up to near the lochans on the saddle. There had been a lot of rain when I was up there, and it was quite boggy going up, so be warned!

From the lochans I tracked round towards the east side to avoid, the old guide said, the very steep north side. There's a broken down wall which tracks up the north east side, and following that up is the best bet. You've got to wonder what they were made of, the men who put the walls there.

The continuation of that same wall is the start of the way down, which is gentler. It takes you westward along the long top, the second withered finger of this so called Awful Hand Range. At the end of the tops, you go off right following a row of iron poles, the remnants of a fence, and this takes you right down to the forestry near Cross Burn. You can get in here to the burn, can be quaggy in places, and you can find the old base of the long gone Wigwam Bothy, marked on the O.S. map as a tiny black square right on the burn. There is no bridge or stepping stones (contrary to old guides) that I could see, so you'll have to just find your best way across. Again, you can't rely on the map in terms of exact forestry layout, and the forestry is dense, the rides often very quaggy. You need to find a way through to the end of the forestry track you set out from. You don't want to be doing this bit as the light is fading, as it's pretty dark in the pine forestry at the best of times. Make sure you leave plenty of time and energy for this short part.

Once on the track, you just have the long trek back to your car.

Time and Difficulty:

Six hours for someone of average fitness. The main dangers I encountered were firstly the ease of getting lost among the ever changing, felled and growing forestry. Also, it's easy to commit yourself to an ever steepening slope near the summit. You always need to be careful crossing water. Getting through dense bits of pine forest, however short, is arduous and disorienting. Finally, I didn't see a soul from leaving the car to returning, apart from the group of deer near the top. Even though it's only the next along in the range from the relatively popular Merrick climb (and this is always quiet compared with the teeming Lakes), it feels far more remote. Absolutely essential to leave word of where you are going, even if it's just a note at your Hotel or B & B or campsite or wherever.

Kirriereoch

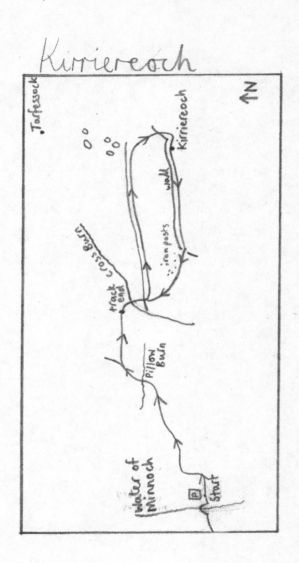

Kirriereoch

I looked up the impossibly steep
grassy slope-
how the grass could even grow there
so neat and trim and sheer.
But my little guide book said
to come right round the back
and avoid the scree on the northern side
and the ominous sounding Green Holes
so there I was looking up at the east side
of the upper slopes of Kirriereoch Hill.
Little Spear and the Merrick to my left,
its Black Gairy looming across,
Lump of the Eglin and Hoodens Hill behind me,
and round Mullwarchar.
And as I gazed up, there, impossible, deer
grazing casual as sheep,
five or six mothers and foals.
So it must be do-able, I thought.
I watched them, their silence,
their concentrated self-absorption,
the first other beings I had seen since I parked.
And they casually monitored me.
When I started up again towards them
inching slowly with stick and step
checking each boot-hold for grip,
the largest one started off
and the others followed without looking back,
keeping their contour on out of sight
through a broken-down dyke.

I stopped and let my sense of them
permeate my body from head to foot
their movement so light so deft
further up this exponential curve of grass.
Only the edges of my sideways feet,
and I tried not to look down
where I knew I couldn't now climb back down
and fleetingly I wondered whether they had appeared
to tempt me up, but I had to stop that kind of thinking,
and just by inching and inching
out of breath and out of shape,
left foot up slope, right foot down,
stick planted between
left hand high, resting on grass
inch by inch to the top.

The curve turned again near the summit
the brim bent over and I looked back down
at what I had done
and where the deer had been
and for a moment wondered
did I see them at all.
No-one else had seen them.
No-one else was there.
And they were so untroubled.

What a strange and beautiful way to be.
Whereas I was tired and sweaty and breathless,
happy and heady and safe after recklessness.
Stones strewn towards the summit
which slopes slowly east to west,
the way I would descend,

the second finger of The Awful Hand.

But first
a picnic in warm September light
thinking about my wife and children,
delicate deer on the dangerous slopes
of a swimming pool in the south of Spain.

I slowly revolved the view
with a sarny in my gob -
to the west I was amazed to see Ailsa Craig
a levitating plum pudding
in a far off sea haze
or a closed sea anemone
detached and still.
Arran and Kintyre just visible beyond.
And at my feet the swathes of thin cheap carpet of pines
and their visible stitch lines.
To the north, Tarfessock and Shalloch on Minnoch
form the two smaller fingers of the Awful Hand,
forestry round Linfern Loch,
big Badan Reservoir and before it Loch Riecaur,
and before that Loch Macaterick with its Blaeberry Isle
past north now the huge Loch Doon in the distance,
east is Hoodens Hill, Mullwarchar and the jelly mould
of Corserine behind. The whole Kells range
looks to me like some mythical beast flying west,
a harpy,
its body Corserine, its head Meikle Craigtarson,
its wings Carlin's Cairn and Meaul to the north,
Millfire and Milldown and Meikle Millyea to the south.
South of me is Merrick's sheer northern face,

the starey dark and white streams of Black Gairy,
and south west more cheap carpet of Glentrool Forest
thin and worn in places,
then the peninsulas - The Machars, and the Mull of Galloway.

The way down is gentler than the way up.
West following a tumble-down wall
then taking to the right along a line
of rusty iron poles with rusty holes,
 all that remains of a long wire fence.
Steeper now down across the wetter lower moors
to Cross Burn where it moves through planted firs
whose rides are boggy after a month of rain.
I am looking for the Wigwam Bothy
pictured in my guide by the side of the burn
but find after some searching
only four steel supports
stubbing out from four concrete founding blocks
and after some searching in the guide
the news that the bothy is long since gone
destroyed by vandals.
I picture schoolkids on trips in the seventies
wearing flares, collecting water from the stream,
camping in a wigwam far from home.

The footbridge near the bothy no longer exists
so I search up and down stream
for a place to cross and for a path
through the forestry the other side.
I jump a narrow fast flowing section
rock to rock
but find only ride after boggy ride,

choose one, get stuck at a fallen tree
with a deep pool under it, go back
and try a few more, really weary now and aware
that if I get hurt here and stuck they might not find me
for weeks, or a year,
or ever,
but that fantasy passes and at last I get up and through
and luckily hit on the big fire break
and turn left and at the end of that
is the hard standing
marking the end of the long track.
It's past six as I step out
in military style
my stick tapping knitted grit
every four strides.

Corserine

To get to the start:

From Newton Stewart, head east over the bridge, onto the B7079, out of town. At the end of this road, turn left onto the A712, signposted New Galloway. About two thirds of the way to New Galloway, just before Clatteringshaws Loch, take a left turn onto a tiny road which takes you a winding way skirting the loch, eventually getting to a gate just before the entrance to the disused Craigencallie Outdoor Centre, with parking space just before the gate.

The Walk:

Continue on foot along this road. Turn right at the next opportunity, signposted left for Loch Dee. Having turned right, you are now, for a few hundred yards, on the Southern Upland Way. Cross the bridge over the River Dee, a.k.a. the Black Water of Dee, very soon, and straight after leave the Southern Upland Way by turning left up the forestry track at a small triangle junction. Follow this track all the way up to the foot of Straverron Hill, passing McWhann's Stone, and bearing right, following the valley of Curnelloch Burn. Where the forestry on your right ends, turn right and make your way up the ride between forestry and where old forestry has been felled some time ago (this boundary is obviously subject to change over time – basically you want to be climbing up the south west side of Straverron Hill, skirting round and up towards Meikle Millyea). It's a good hard steep climb up and onto Meikle Millyea (746m).

Approximately two hours from the start, for someone of average fitness. Great views from here on a clear day.

Next you head a little east of north along the Rhinns of Kells, the undulating ridge along which you can pick off the summits of the Kells Range. Take care to know where you are, as the east and north east sides of these hills are very steep, particularly Milldown (738m). Craigeazle (449m), which looked sizeable as you walked along forestry tracks in the valley, is now small below you, and beyond it the magnificent sheer sides of the Dungeon Range. Snibe Hill, Craignaw, Dungeon Hill itself. In good light, before the sun comes right over, these sheer sides shine in an extraordinary way. With flat marshland and the Round Loch of the Dungeon and the Long Loch of the Dungeon below them, and with the Merrick behind, this view is stupendous.

You go down past the Lochans of Auchniebut, and up to Milldown (738m), down and up again to Millfire (716m), and finally down and gradually up onto the long slow slopes of the south side of Corserine (814m). If you've loads of energy left, go on to Carlin's Cairn (807m) and back. Maybe next time I'll make it that far. Either way, from Corserine now go west, down and up to Meikle Craigtarson (620m). Drop down the (steep) south west side, picking carefully through felled forestry stumps, and disused pits near the bottom. Take the forestry track left all the way past the Backhill of Bush Bothy, situated idyllically on Downies Burn, under the steep sides of Dungeon Hill and Craignaw. Continue as the road, more open than the map shows, presumably due to recent felling, follows parallel to Cooran Lane, then swings left to meet your original path just after crossing Curnelloch Burn, just before McWhann's Stone.

69

Now retrace those first steps back, turning right at the triangle, across the River Dee, then left leaving the Southern Upland Way again, back to your car.

Time and Difficulty:

A good seven hours for me, and I'd say I'm of average fitness. By no means a hardened hiker. This walk and the Loch Enoch one really took me to my limit. Although from the foot of Meikle Craigtarson, the long walk back is pretty much flat. Roughly twelve miles, without visiting Carlin's Cairn. You can, if you wish, take a shorter circuit. If, just after the summit of Milldown, you follow the wall which goes down left, east, through forestry and following Downies Burn, to Backhill of Bush Bothy. You'd still have had those great views from the Rhinns of Kells.

Corserine

Meikle Craigtarson   Corserine

↑N

Backhill
of Bush Bothy

RHINNS OF KELLS

Millfire

Milldown

Meikle
Millyea

Burn

Corran Lane

Curnelloch

McWhann's
Stone

Loch
Dee

Start

Craigencattie

71

Corserine

I parked in a passing place before a gate
near the site of a disused outdoor centre,
Craigencallie House, in a state of disrepair,
the centre and myself,
nature almost gone from me,
nature making inroads on the house.

I walked on up the track,
a slow curve through forestry
between the close hills
of Cairngarroch and Darrou
then turned right
joining the Southern Upland Way
for a few hundred yards
as it crossed the Bridge over the River Dee -
thinking of Alec Guinness -
the Bridge over the Black Water of Dee,
and the water was black and frilling and wide
and the scene could have been Canada or the U.S.A.

The dark waters of Loch Dee out of sight
for a few hours yet
but some of it passing the bridge
mixed with Curnelloch Burn and Cooran Lane
and Green Burn and Cleugh Burn and Black Strand
and Downies Burn, and Brishie Burn bringing water
from the Round Loch of the Dungeon
and the Long Loch of the Dungeon.

The water was dark and the water was cold
and the rapids frilled white as I stood on the bridge.

On the far side I went left, leaving The Way
and went on up the forestry road
past McWhann's Stone and the Rig of Divots,
Little Millyea to my right,
Craigeazle and tops of Craigeazle
making a small ridge of grassy
and craggy knolls
on and to the left of me.
Opposite the foot of Craigeazle, I struck right
along the end of forestry, steeply up a wet ride
beyond which the trees had been cropped some years ago,
rows of stumps, the odd pole left standing,
some kind of marker,
looking like a lone standard after a massacre,
thick couch grass or some such
hiding most of the lumps in the ground.

When the trees ended I skirted right,
round Straverron Hill
and attained the zenith of Meikle Millyea
by twelve noon.
As I climbed, the Dungeon Range – Snibe Hill,
Craignaw, Dungeon Hill itself,
came into view beyond Craigeazle
their sheer east sides silver,
a light beyond description,
a sign of fixity and flow.
I sat and ate and felt new.
I went to text my wife in Spain

but I couldn't send,
there was not even emergency
coverage on my phone
it's 02, which used to be Cellnet,
which was part of BT
which always had the best coverage,
I remember from selling mobile phones.
I felt wonderful and wild and free.

I looked southwest down to black Loch Dee
and east to St John's Town of Dalry
and headed off north along the Rhinns of Kells
descending to the Lochans of Auchniebut
and ascending to Milldown
following the farmers' quadbike tracks
but seeing no sheep
up and down the ridge all the way
past Millfire and onto the long slopes
of Corserine.

A middle aged couple walking well apart
passed me going the other way,
the only souls I had seen that day,
carefully planting their ski-pole sticks.
After a while I turned
and watched them becoming dots,
and it made me think of Immanuel Kant,
and Plato's cave, and The Third Man.
Not that I have ever got round
to actually reading Kant.
I still have a copy of the Critique,
but it is moving down the long slide

to endlessness.

By the top of Corserine my legs were jelly
on the great green jelly mould
and I decided to leave Carlin's Cairn, beyond,
for another day,
like Kant,
turned west towards Meikle Craigtarson,
a long rollercoaster curve
down through deep and springy grass
and up over short-cropped turf and stones,
descended then its steepish southern side
past disused pits and awkward
outcrops of stone and stumps
to the forest road below.
These roads are laid hardcore,
sometimes with grit on top,
and they wind their way through the forestry
of the valley floors.

Finally the long trudge back the stony road
past Backhill of Bush bothy on Downies Burn
under the cliffs of Craignaw and Dungeon Hill,
the light gone from them now.
The bothy cottage a concentration of emptiness,
plain and simple and small.
Walking away the long open road from the bothy
I felt less heavy in my fatigue
I felt small and marvellously insignificant,
as when one gazes on a storm-shouldering sea,
small, but implicated in enormity.

It was a long walk in the valley of Cooran Lane,
and the miles were flat but slow.
And without having to place each step, at last,
with a steady walking rhythm
and with total knackeredness, comes
a change in mental processes, a shift,
as when a sailing dinghy begins to plane.
The helm, the sheets, everything becomes lighter.
And though you are moving faster,
everything slows down.
At the bottom of the valley of Cooran Lane
my path down met my path up
and I passed McWhann's Stone again
and on down to the Bridge over the River Dee,
the Bridge over the Black Water of Dee,
and all of the water was different now
and all of the water was the same,
frilling white on black in the same places,
in the same form.
It could have been the U.S.A. or Canada.
Trudging wobbly now only the rhythm
of walking keeping the walking on.
At the car I was glad I'd already
turned the car around,
I drove slowly back past a logger's wasteland -
a tiny caravan, a car, an empty wagon,
its red steel posts sticking up in air.
I drove round the fringes of Clatterinshaws Loch
heading home.

Cairnsmore of Fleet

To get to the start:

From Newton Stewart take the A75 eastbound, then turn left, the next one after the Palnure turn and after the bridge over Palnure burn. The left turn you're looking for is only a few hundred yards further on, and is not signposted. Follow this lane past a few cottages, past a private entrance which goes in through an arch in the disused railway. Shortly after, you see a parking sign, where you turn right, and park in one of the little bays.

The Walk:

This is an ideal first large hill walk. The path is well marked all the way (except in exceptional conditions – see the Cairnsmore 2 poem). Oh, and there's no marked path across the field near the start. The going is steady, never ridiculously steep. Having said that, it is worth noting that although Cairnsmore of Fleet (711m) is not quite as high as Merrick (843m) or Corserine (814m), the car park from which you start is virtually at sea level, whereas for those other walks you park at 150m (Loch Trool), and 200m (Craigencallie). So although generally smooth and steady up this big blob of a hill, you are going up and down further than you might think.

To start you go left at the far end of the car park, following the driveway of the never glimpsed grand house. Near the end of this road, before you get to the old stables of the house, there's

a sign for the hill walk, taking you right, so that you skirt round these stables which have been converted into dwellings. Old guides will tell you to drive right up and past the stables, parking at a picnic area beyond them. You can no longer do this. The walk skirts round, signed left soon, and once round the back of these properties, you pass the picnic area with its No Parking sign. Don't be disheartened or put off by all the negative Private No Entry, No Parking, Beware The Bull, Cows With Calves, Fields May Contain Grass, Watch Out For Trolls, etc. ... It is your land too, after all.

Continue diagonally up through the field, and behind gorse at the far corner, which when in flower has a lovely scent of coconut. Find the gate to the path, which takes you up through forestry. There's an option of a different walk shortly, a left hand turn signposted Mill Burn Path. I've not been down this but it's one to consider if you or the kids are already struggling a bit at this stage. My eldest son completed the Cairnsmore walk with me when he was seven, but he is very fit and sporty. There's no way I could have done it until I was fifteen or so. Know your limitations, and those of your group!

It's a long steady slog up through pine forestry now. About halfway , you cross a track. Just beyond that, in a location with a great view back down over the Cree, and the Machar peninsula beyond, there's a marble bench. It's one of those which are half a huge boulder, the cuts through which are smooth and curved, forming your seat. It's not at all a bad place for a snack and to get a sense of how high you've already come.

Continue a bit steeper now, until you come out onto the moorland proper. Follow the path, fairly flat, across heather, to a stile, and move now onto the most testing part, winding up through a broken down dry stone wall, all the way to the top. Even as the path levels off somewhat, you still have a fair distance to go. Keep on, and just before the summit cairn, there's a memorial to those who died in plane crashes on the hill in World War Two. The plaque, which has had to be replaced once, has had further attempts to deface it. It memorialises the German dead here as well as the Allied.

Wonderful views on a clear day.

Time and Difficulty:

Five hours, approximately, for average walkers. That's with several stops, and a bite of lunch at the top. Roughly eight miles in all. Definitely the least arduous way to get views like these.

Cairnsmore of Fleet 1

At the beginning
the way is the grand driveway
up towards a hidden mansion house
with a stream on the right
and mature planted trees, as you would expect.
There's a large one recently felled
or fallen
and a huge trunk
a chunky rough cylinder
lies next to the stump.
The brashings have mostly been moved or processed
but the trunk will just be left,
too expensive to process.

The road curves right
where the gated way to the house
goes left,
just after a field that is almost parkland
with a few massive oaks,
which are fenced but where
there are no longer deer.

The largest oak
with all the room it needs and more
has spread wide and high.
It has pathos and I think the pathos
has something to do with time
and human vanity.
Like the pathos of a self-published book.

The first time we came here
was with buggy and toddler
and all the paraphernalia
and that tree was as far as we got
after twenty minutes of uphill whinge from the boys
resisting every attempt to trick -
the fox around the next corner,
the deer, the Gruffalo, the squirrel.

My daughter and I gained the summit a year later -
on that driveway we saw a red squirrel
scarper straight up a tree
so small and feisty and flirty,
its brush flicking,
its coat immaculate and bright.

Tentatively through the gate,
with its warning of a bull
which years later became a warning
about cows with calves.

After the first field it's firs,
a long ascent,
pauses to look back over the Cree
and the Cree's estuary,
and the Machars peninsular,
relatively flat land laid out,
some real meanders.

There's a bench of marble,
inscribed, and, near it

a rack of incongruous paddles
for forest fires.
The stone is cut in a smooth curve
but the rest is still rough boulder.
Where you sit used to be boulder.

Quite a lot further up we emerged
onto open hillside,
the long path clear ahead, to a stile,
then heading off steeper round and up.
We were shocked to see what remained
laid out before us,
and when I saw on the map our lowly contour,
we stopped to picnic.

South east I saw
the notches of Cairnharrow
and beneath them Cambret Hill
with its satellite dishes
and television mast and mobile phone masts.
North west the long ridge
of what must be Drigmore Hill,
Millfore, Cairngarroch.
The more distant Larg Hill and Lamachan
maybe make up
the left hand end
of what we can see.
The map tells us what we see
and helps us see. Hills slowly
individuate.

As we sat we spotted two moving dots,

climbers way ahead of us,
and we started to think maybe we could make it.

Slow and steady, short steps, I tell her,
as my father used to tell me,
more out of breath myself,
as he himself had been more out of breath.
And she ignores me
with her long legged stride,
just as I ignored his advice.

The gradient gets progressively steeper.
And then when finally it starts to flatten off
we still have a lot further to go than we think.

It's a big long old lump of a thing, Cairnsmore.
Just before the summit we see a memorial
to airmen who crashed here during the war.
The original plaque on the stone has been replaced
and some attempt has been made
to deface the German names on the new one.

We are elated to be there and don't yet know
how aching and jelly-wobbly
our legs will be going down.
We add a few stones to the huge cairn
and see to our surprise,
bees, lots of bees, slow and close
round the cairn which must hold their hive.

Cairnsmore 2

Today I climbed through the finest powder snow
laid last night on top of three-day-old stuff.
Blue sky, brisk wind.
The firs whooshing, almost wailing,
and up on the open moors,
powder blown like a mad low mist a foot high
hither and thithering fast
through bits of protruding heather,
and behind each bit a slipstream of drift,
a mazy and alien landscape.

But I didn't make the summit.
I gave up beyond the stile,
beyond the broken down dyke further up,
after I lost the path and was hampered by big drifts,
my stick disappearing,
after I'd re-found the path and lost it again
and had one last push.
But higher up the powder was moving fast
and the weather could change
and the blood was bumping too fast in my head
and other excuses.

A View of Loch Dee

To get to the start:

From Newton Stewart take the A714 north, turn right at Bargrennan, signposted to Glentrool. At Glentrool village, turn right, signposted to Loch Trool. This road takes you to Stroan Bridge. Park at the visitor centre just beyond it.

The Walk:

This a good, long, fairly flat walk, with a view of Loch Dee before you turn back.

It's the sort of route people used for thousands of years to get about on foot. Tracking along rivers, keeping to contours, going through passes. So you're getting much more of an ancient feel of the terrain than on the hill walks.

From the car park, follow the small path down along the Water of Minnoch. It bears left at the confluence of the Minnoch and the Water of Trool, tracking up along the Water of Trool. Turn right to cross the Water of Trool via a sturdy wooden footbridge. Now turn left, joining the Southern Upland Way. The path takes you along the river to the loch which feeds it. Just before you get to Loch Trool, there is a short path spur off to the right, to a Covenanters' monument, at the site where six men, caught at prayer, were shot dead. Returning to the main path, you soon reach Caldons. Shortened versions of this walk can start here, parking being available the other side of the river, off the main

Loch Trool road. You can do a simple loop of Loch Trool, or extend it to see Loch Dee as in this walk.

Go straight on past Caldons - the path keeps a distance from the house there, and then follows tight along the steep south shore of the loch, past the site of the Battle of Glentrool (1307). Continue past the end of the loch, and go right, just before a footbridge and on, passing near another bridge which looks like a piece of a Second World War pontoon. Follow the forestry track up through the pass until you get a great view of Loch Dee and the hills beyond. Turn back now, but go right and over the military-style bridge, pass Glenhead, and the path takes you over the feet of Gairland Burn and then Buchan Burn at Buchan Bridge and up to the Bruce's Stone car park. Now follow the road down past the entrance way to Glen Trool Lodge, then three quarters of a mile beyond this, take a left to Caldons, over the bridge and right, onto the Southern Upland Way, retracing your steps back down the Water of Trool, over the wooden footbridge, then up along the Minnoch to the Stroan Bridge Car Park.

Time and Difficulty:

Total distance about twelve miles. Time, about four and a half hours, for someone of average fitness. Always allow extra time. If you just do the loop round Loch Trool from Caldons Car Park it's about five miles. Extending that to see Loch Dee adds another three miles. All these options are a lot easier on the legs than the hill walks, and have a good path all the way.

Another variant, if you are being dropped off and picked up, is to be dropped at Stroan Bridge, and picked up at Craigencallie outdoor centre. Simply continue on along the Southern Upland Way past Loch Dee, turning right, leaving the Southern Upland Way, just before the Bridge over the River Dee. This road takes you to the parking place, hard standing just beyond a gate, near the entrance to the disused Craigencallie Outdoor Centre. This route is also roughly twelve miles. Again, you can shorten it by starting at Caldons or Loch Trool Car Park. And of course you could do it the other direction, starting off at Craigencallie.

A view of Loch Dee

N

view

Loch
Trool

P

⨉ 1307

F. Water of Trool

F.B.

Start
P

Stroan
Bridge

Water of Minnoch

91

Loch Dee

In snow silence I stand still
absorbing the hills.
I have been walking for four hours
the sun is low somewhere
and this hillside next to me
faces south so its snow is mostly gone.
And now in late light its bracken
and its heather glows
hypnotic, hallucinogenic brown.

I left my car at Stroan Bridge-
the road to Loch Trool was inches thick ice
so I walked and hobbled from there
down the roadside with my stick a couple of miles
then turned right, following the Southern Upland Way
round the south side of the loch
past the scene of the Battle of Glentrool.
And on up past Glenhead
following a forestry road
steadily up through the pass
between Corse Knowe of Glenhead
and Corse Knowe of White Laggan
until I got sight of the frozen Loch Dee.

As it emerged over the brow
I stopped, quiet,
but for the blood bumping in my head.
I could see what you see on a hot summer's day
over hot tarmac

making what's beyond it waver
and seem insubstantial.

And as the blood in my head slowly calmed down
it was still there and slowly I realised
I wasn't seeing things, become too tired,
hallucinating a memory.
It was just convection currents in the air
just a heat differential
the sun low somewhere but strong
amongst this ice and snow.

It still felt weird to look at it
and the words sound odd,
'heat haze',
with behind it, Loch Dee locked up in ice,
its two small incursions of land
and its island with a single tree.

I could see Meikle Millyea
distant and snow-smothered,
Little Millyea and Darrou nearer.

To get back to the car by dark
I had to turn away now, but I had seen
Loch Dee frozen over
and wondered if I ever would again.
What with kids and work and all that.

Without striking a keening note,
I wouldn't want that,
a man could die happy

having stood where I stood
alone in that scene
ready to turn and return,
still, in the snow silence,
hearing only the tiny sound
of a distant, nearly frozen stream.

Loch Enoch

To get to the start:

From Newton Stewart take the A714 north, turn right at Bargrennan, signposted to Glentrool. At Glentrool village, turn right, signposted to Loch Trool. Go straight on past Stroan Bridge visitor centre a further couple of miles, to the Loch Trool car park, which has two parts.

An alternative route from Newton Stewart is to take the slower, but even more picturesque Minigaff road. Cross the bridge over the Cree from the main town centre of Newton Stewart, onto the B7079, then turn left, signed Minigaff. Turn left again, signed Wood of Cree. The road takes you up parallel to the A714, but across the Cree from it, on the eastern side, and closer to the river. It's a lovely drive. At the end of the road you turn right, to the Stroan Bridge Visitor Centre, which you pass, heading on to the car park at Bruce's Stone, the north side of Loch Trool.

The Walk:

It's a long loop of a walk. You need to be reasonably fit. Lots of climbs and descents, tiring on the legs. But absolutely worth it.

Once parked, follow the mettled road on past the car park, down past Buchan Bridge. Soon after, take the second path off up to the left, clearly marked Gairland Burn and Loch Neldricken. The path skirts round Buchan Hill, and follows Gairland Burn up to Loch Valley. Follow the path along the east side of Loch Valley, then, at an old sheepfold, find stepping stones to cross the Mid Burn.

Anywhere along Gairland Burn is an idyllic place for a picnic, though it's usually a bit boggy as you approach Loch Valley. The crossing point of the Mid Burn is as far as I'd go with little ones. There's no path from here, and the going gets a lot harder.

Strike east now with no path, up to an unnamed summit (493m), and on to the top of Snibe Hill (533m). Then turn north to head down and up to Craignaw (645m), through grassy corridors in the rock. There are often mountain goats in this area. They keep their distance, but it's always worth being mindful of them and their young. The east sides of Snibe Hill and Craignaw, in fact of all the Dungeon Range, are pretty sheer. You do not want to be up there without a compass and map if the weather closes in. The way up to Craignaw's summit is very craggy, with huge slabs of rock strewn around. Staggering views if it's clear. The summit of Craignaw is the last point from which it will be quicker to return the way you came, rather than to carry on. Going down over the far side is tricky, the most difficult bit of this walk. You have to pick your route carefully. Go via the cairn at the top of the Nick of the Dungeon, from where you have the option to follow a path up to scale Dungeon Hill (610m) if you've plenty left in the tank, or go up Craignairny (595m), then on, to Craig Neldricken (552m). There are guides which recommend then keeping the high ground round south west to go along the top of the Rig of Loch Enoch, Craignine, and Buchan Hill (493m). However, in the walk described in the accompanying poem, I wanted to go down to Loch Enoch, apparently the highest loch in Scotland (500m), and in any case I couldn't see a way from Craig Neldricken onto the Rig of Loch

Enoch without the sort of climbing which, in my state of fatigue, I didn't feel up to. You've always got to be prepared to use your common sense. So my chosen route is to drop down from Craig Neldricken to the south west corner of Loch Enoch, a remote and peaceful place, and less exposed than the tops. From here you can follow a wall through the pass all the way under the west side of the Rig of Loch Enoch and Craignine and Buchan Hill. The going is heavy, stick to the high side where you can. Watch out for holes. You then need to cross Buchan Burn at some point. I cross about half a mile north of the car park, where the path for the Merrick climb is very close the other side, then follow that path down to the car. (You could skirt right round Buchan Hill and join the Gairland burn path you started on, or join up with the path which goes up the east side of Buchan Burn. Weather conditions, and the state of the ground, your level of experience, and your state of tiredness will dictate your choice). I certainly knew I'd overdone it by the time I'd got to Loch Enoch. But there's no quick way back from there! However, I have been sustained for months by the experience of that walk. The small herds of mountain goats, the views, the sense of isolation and stillness. And then my encounter with a stag.

Time and Difficulty:

The walk took me seven hours. I am of average fitness. The four peaks in the middle of the walk take it out of you with the constant up and down. And it's always harder and slower without a path. It's more than worth the effort though, as the top of Craignaw is about as craggy and remote as it gets in the Galloway Hills. You have Merrick and the Awful Hand Range on one side, and the Kells Range on the other.

Loch Enoch

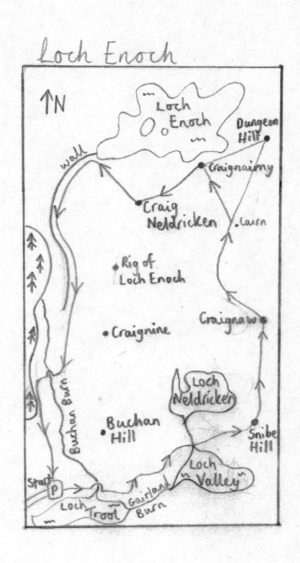

↑N

Loch Enoch

Dungeon Hill

wall

Craignairny

Craig Neldricken

cairn

Rig of Loch Enoch

Craignine

Craignaw

Loch Neldricken

Buchan Hill

Snibe Hill

Buchan Burn

Loch Valley

Sprue

P

Loch Trool

Gairland Burn

Loch Enoch

By the time my peripheral vision
had picked up a movement or odd form
and turned my head,
he must have been watching me a while.

He was still, not chewing any more.
Dark, thick-set shaggy shoulders.
Antlers like dark mistletoe.

I was exhausted from a long day's walking,
had only a couple of miles to go
back to my car
but my legs were sore, looser, wobbly,
and I was aware
that my judgment had gone wonky.
I kept being tempted to try to cross the boggy land
below this half broken-down dry stone wall
I had been using as my guide.
Then I'd get stuck
and have to work back up to and over the wall
to continue.

I had started my hike
following the footpath by the Gairland Burn
round the side of Buchan Hill to Loch Valley.
The stream had fizzed in the September sun.
I crossed the Mid Burn
between Loch Valley and Loch Neldricken
using stepping stones next to an old sheepfold.

I climbed up to the top of Snibe Hill,
had lunch
and could see across low ground to Corserine
where I'd walked a few days before.

Then I moved on, down and up, north, to Craignaw
past groups of mountain goats
with great sweeping horns
and little kids,
through an all-pervading goaty musk
like, well, like goat's cheese.
They stood on high rocky outcrops in the sun
and I walked through the grassy
corridors between them.

Huge slabs and crags all the way up.
The almost sheer east side,
which I had seen silvering from the Rhinns of Kells
falling away to my right.
It was hard going up
and harder work over and down the far side,
and I was glad of my stick,
which steadied me when I disturbed a grouse
that clattered out terrified
squawking suddenly
from a foot away,
as gingerly I climbed down a crag,
step, tap, step.

And it helped me as I eased my way
round the Nick of the Dungeon
up onto Craignairny.

On the Devil's Bowling Green
I surprised two hikers
headed the opposite way.
I loomed like wildlife -
they had thought they had the place
to themselves.

From Craignairny I could see Loch Enoch,
Its strange shape with its many
land incursions and its islands,
and I could see the white sand of its little beaches,
which I'd heard was very fine,
and used to be prized for sharpening blades.

I was getting weary in my legs.
Down and up to Craig Neldricken,
and down to the south-west
corner of the loch,
where I leaned through a rusty wire fence
collected a few pinches of the sand,
and considered the start of a sad refrain.

I followed a wall
which led up through a small pass, then down,
(looking at the O.S. map), skirted the west side
of the Rig of Loch Enoch, and of Craignine
towards where, a few miles on,
I could cross Buchan Burn
and join the end of another path
back to my car.

It was as the wall skirted round Craignine
that I came upon the stag.
He was halfway across the boggy bit
between the patchy wall and me
and the pine wood -
about a hundred yards -
and the forestry was fenced.

So he stood
sniffing the air
looking at me, through me
and now, given that I was still,
I wonder if he could see me at all,
but at the time I just looked -
he was an awesome sight -
and I wondered if he might
think that I might
shoot him.

So tired and without thought
I called out
thinking to reassure him
something pathetic like
'It's o.k. staggy stag I won't harm you,
I'm just here for a walk'.
As though I were in control.
You know, towny-dad crap,
except my kids weren't there for excuse.
They were in Spain with their mum and grandad,
they were running across the top of the pool,
taking the cheap week off school.

My stupid noise
gave him the jitters
and he jolted then moved like a wave
down to the fence,
nimble flow across ground where I'd got stuck.
He turned back
as if to check,
then affirming something in himself
jumped the fence
twanging it with his hind legs
but never losing his poise,
and by the time the sound reached me
he was disappeared into the pines.